You're Gonna Be Okay

Truth, Practices, and Encouragement to Give You Hope When You Feel Hopeless

Rev. Susan Eaton

Stewart Eaton, LPC, CSAT

ISBN: 978-0-578-71505-6 (Paperback)

For Will and Rachel:

Being your parents is the most rewarding work we have ever done. May you always know how much you are loved by God and by us, and may the joy of the Lord always be your strength.

CONTENTS

ADDITIONAL RESOURCES

HOW TO USE THIS BOOK

This book was written to serve as a loving companion and practical guide to help you navigate the darkness of depression and anxiety. In these pages you'll find scriptural passages and readings along with prayers, journaling prompts, and links to music.

Even on your lowest days, we encourage you to pick up this book and work through at least one passage of Scripture and the reading that goes along with it. We know from personal experience that it can be very challenging to want to read anything when you are feeling depressed or anxious, or to even know where to begin with prayer. This book will give you easy access to Scriptures that offer the comfort, strength, and wisdom you need, while also providing specific prayers and other prompts to help you develop your own spiritual muscles.

Journaling

You'll notice that some of the readings include journaling prompts and questions to guide you. Feel free to write in this book, or keep a private journal handy to write in as you heal. You may find that you want to express yourself through writing as you read the Scriptures and engage with the questions. We encourage this wholeheartedly.

Writing can serve as an extremely healing way to process emotions. Writing in stream of consciousness style to the

Lord is one of my favorite ways to pray. In fact, some of the prayers in this book were written as I (Susan) sat in the quiet and wrote to the Lord in my private journal.

Music

Music can be a beautiful way to connect with the Lord when our minds are crowded and our bodies are stressed. We're wired to retain the messages of a song differently than the written word. In addition, calming music is healing for both body and soul. That's why we have suggested songs for most of the readings. If you don't resonate with these particular songs, or if you prefer instrumental music, find music that works best for you and let it lead you into the presence of the Lord.

A note about the music links

If you are using an ebook version, just click the title of each song. We have included QR codes for those using the printed version of this book. Depending on the type of device you are using, you may need to download a QR code reader first to scan the codes. Most iPhone users should be able to scan the code using their phone camera.

Resource list in the back

We have included links to helpful resources in the back of this book that you'll want to check out. These resources will help you understand more about depression, anxiety, breathing practices, relaxation techniques, and so much more. They include quality resources Stewart has used in his practice with teens, young adults, and families. We also hope the Q&A section will give you guidance on any next steps you may need to take in terms of finding additional support.

A note to parents

If you are a parent whose teen is struggling, give a copy to your teen and keep one for yourself. You may choose to read a passage daily with your teen and discuss the readings with him or her, or you may choose to read separately and talk with your teen about it later. Either way, we hope these readings will serve as a conversation starter between you and your son or daughter.

Whoever you are, please know that if you are reading this book, you have been prayed for immensely. Our hope and prayer is that you will encounter the Lord[1] in a powerful way as you enter into his presence. We are rooting for you, and the Lord is always on your side. You are not alone. May your peace and healing come quickly.

---

[1] Throughout this book we've referred to God as a male entity, using the pronouns he, him, and his. We've done this for simplicity's sake and because it's the most common style used in pulications. However, we recognize the painful trauma wounds that can be triggered when abuse survivors are taught to picture God as a man. For this reason, we encourage you to envision God in the way that feels right to your hearts. The truth is, God is undefinable, so no words will ever be able to adequately capture the infinite love, wisdom, and power he offers this world.

INTRODUCTION

When I feel threatened or burdened, I look to models of courage in the Scriptures. One striking story stands out as my husband and I write this book.

In 1 Kings 18:20-40, the prophet Elijah experiences a showdown. You see, King Ahab of Israel had done what no king of Israel was supposed to do: He'd married someone who worshiped false gods. Jezebel, Ahab's wife, worshiped the god Baal, among others, and soon the people of Israel began to incorporate worship of Baal into their lives while continuing to worship Yahweh[2], the God of Israel.

This behavior was in direct opposition to the covenant God's people had made with him at Mount Sinai (see Exodus 20:3-6). Elijah showed extreme faith and stunning courage as he stood against the four-hundred and fifty prophets of Baal and proved in very dramatic fashion (seriously, go read 1 Kings 18:20-40) that Baal was a fake: Yahweh was the one true God. When the LORD[3] showed himself to be present, powerful, and real, the people of Israel hit the ground and repeated this truth: *"The LORD indeed is God; the LORD indeed is God."*

---

[2] Yahweh is a form of the Hebrew name of God used in the Bible.

[3] Fun fact: When you see the word "LORD" printed in all caps it is specifically referring to the Hebrew name for God, Yahweh.

When Ahab reported to his wife, Jezebel, what Elijah had done, she became so angry that she swore to kill Elijah by the same time the next day (1 Kings 19:2). Fearing for his life, Elijah fled with his servant to a place called Beersheba. He left his servant there and traveled a day's journey into the wilderness.

Now, doesn't that seem strange? Why would Elijah, who had just shown so much courage, strength, and faith, be so overwhelmed by fear? I don't know the answer to that. Nothing in the text tells us why he was so afraid. It just says that he was, which tells me something important: Fear can affect anyone. If a man like Elijah could feel helpless, vulnerable, and weak, it makes sense that we could have that experience, too.

After traveling a full day, Elijah came to a solitary broom tree and sat down to rest. In his exhaustion, Elijah prayed and asked that he might die. *"I have had enough, Lord,"* he said. *"Take my life, for I am no better than my ancestors who have already died"* (1 Kings 19:4). Elijah, the man who had just experienced the miraculous power of the LORD, became so depressed, fearful, and dejected that he prayed for the LORD to end his life. With these desperate and distorted thoughts clouding his mind, Elijah lay down under the broom tree and fell asleep.

Was this the end of Elijah? Was he really better off dead? Was there no hope for him? No, not at all. The LORD would use this pain to bring him into a place of healing. As I've heard it said, breakdowns often lead to breakthroughs.

5 Then he lay down and slept under the broom tree. But as he was sleeping, an angel touched him and told him, "Get up and eat!" 6 He looked around and there beside his head was some bread baked on hot stones and a jar of water! So he ate and drank and lay down again. 7 Then the angel of the Lord came again and touched him and said, "Get up and eat some more, or the journey ahead will be too much for you." 8 So he got up and ate and drank, and the food gave him enough strength to travel forty days and forty nights to Mount Horeb, the mountain of God. 9 There he came to a cave, where he spent the night. (1 Kings 19:4-9a)

In his deepest depression and utter exhaustion—physical, emotional, and spiritual exhaustion—Elijah was not alone. He was seen, he was loved, and he was provided for. The nourishment of physical rest and food, along with the presence and loving care of the LORD, enabled Elijah to get up and keep going. He went in the strength of that food for forty days and forty nights until he reached Mount Horeb. And it was there on this mountain that Elijah had another dramatic encounter with Yahweh. The LORD spoke to Elijah and instructed him: *"Go stand on the mountain before the LORD, for the LORD is about to pass by."*

Elijah did as the LORD instructed, when suddenly he was overwhelmed by wind and earthquake and fire! But the LORD was not in any of that. After the chaos passed, however, there was a sound of sheer silence—a silence so profound that Elijah sensed the presence of the LORD in his midst. *"When Elijah heard it, he wrapped his face in his mantle and went out and stood at the entrance of the cave."* The voice of the LORD came to Elijah, spoke truth into his heart, mind, and soul, and reminded him that **he was not alone.** *(*1 Kings 19:9-18).

What enabled Elijah to recover from what may have been the most emotionally and spiritually distressing time in his life? An encounter with the LORD. The LORD spoke against the fear and lies and filled Elijah with the truth that he was not alone. He comforted and strengthened him like only God could do.

It was the LORD's presence that commanded the chaos to cease because the LORD is not the God of chaos, but the God of peace. In His presence, chaos is stilled, lies are exposed, and peace and truth manifest. In the presence of the LORD Elijah found the strength to carry on.

But before this personal encounter with God at Mount Horeb, the bread and water fed Elijah and gave him the boost he needed to make his journey into the presence of God. That's what this book is intended to be: nourishment for your soul and mind— truth and practices that can help you enter into a place of rest where you can be strengthened and encouraged. But the real work happens in the presence of God, and only you can take that journey.

If you have been feeling lost and unsure of how to connect with the LORD, our hope and prayer is that this book can give you the nourishment you need to journey to him. Get up. Eat. Drink. Fill your heart and mind with the nourishing truth of the LORD. Then notice how the chaos inside you stills, and listen. Because out of the silence, the LORD will speak and you will know— *you're gonna be okay.*

1 Peter 5:6-11

Humble yourselves under the mighty hand of God, so that he may exalt you in due time. Cast all your anxiety on him, because he cares for you. Discipline yourselves, keep alert. Like a roaring lion your adversary the devil prowls around looking for someone to devour. Resist him, steadfast in your faith, for you know that your brothers and sisters in all the world are undergoing the same kinds of suffering. And after you have suffered for a little while, the God of all grace, who has called you to his eternal glory in Christ, will himself restore, support, strengthen and establish you. To him be the power forever and ever. Amen.

A Prayer for Redemption and Wholeness

You, Lord, are my Rock and my Redeemer, my Fortress. You are my Joy and Sunshine. You never change. You always desire good and from you comes our healing and restoration. You know how to heal and redeem in this life, and you know how to bring us whole and complete into eternal life in your presence.

I'm clinging to this truth, Lord—clinging to you. When everything else around me is out of my control and cracking and breaking, you are the same strong, loving and able God who holds the whole world in your hands.

Help me remember that I am one you have created. You have created me to live a FULL life. Shower your love upon me, Lord, so that I can truly love myself.

Defeat the enemy that seeks to devour me—the enemy that speaks lies and creates distortions in my mind. Devour him, Lord, and do not let him devour me. Bring me whole and complete through this wilderness I am in.

If Jonah can come out of the belly of a whale…

If your people can return home from exile…

If you can call Lazarus out of the tomb…

If you can return to life and breathe your Spirit into your people…

…then you can heal and resurrect me from this pit that is seeking to swallow me.

In the name of Jesus, my Savior, I pray.

Amen.

LISTEN
To the End, by Mack Brock
Scan QR code to listen on Spotify[4]

---

[4] You will need to create a Spotify account to listen to the songs linked through the QR codes. You can create a free Spotify account quickly and easily at **https://www.spotify.com** . With a free account the codes linked here will take you to the full album. In order to go straight to the tracks that are linked, you need a Spotify Premium account.

—

When Things Seem Impossible

Psalm 91:1-4; 14-16

"You who live in the shelter of the Most High, who abide in the shadow of the Almighty, will say to the LORD, 'My refuge and my fortress; my God, in whom I trust.' For he will deliver you from the snare of the fowler and from the deadly pestilence; he will cover you with his pinions, and under his wings you will find refuge; his faithfulness is a shield and buckler.

"Those who love me, I will deliver; I will protect those who know my name. When they call to me, I will answer them; I will be with them in trouble, I will rescue them and honor them. With long life I will satisfy them, and show them my salvation."

When things seem impossible remember: God is the God of impossible things. The Lord loves doing the "impossible!"

God created the world, the whole universe, everything in creation, OUT OF NOTHING.

God rescued millions of people from slavery in Egypt through one man, Moses—a man who was a "convict" and who had a stutter. Yet, he led God's people out of Egypt and kept them together in the midst of a forty-year stint in the wilderness. God did that through one man who never imagined himself doing anything of the sort.

Jesus brought back a little girl from the dead—not to mention Lazarus who had been in the tomb for four days!

"IMPOSSIBLE!" some would say.

But, you see, nothing is impossible with God.

This valley you are in may seem endless. It may be so dark that you can't fathom seeing light again or feeling light again.

But nothing is impossible with God.

Whether it was healing people of crippling diseases, walking on water, or rising from the dead, Jesus proved that with God all things are possible.

Don't give up.
Don't give in.
Don't lose hope.

Nothing is impossible with God.

This valley will not have the last word. God has the last word! "Rise!" "Get up!" "Be healed!" "Come out!" Your God sees you. He is El Roi, "God who sees." He is really good at seeing in the dark.

Your God loves you. The LORD is your Shelter, your Shepherd, your Healer, your Comforter who is always present with you. There is no place the LORD won't go to rescue you. God is never worried, never scared, and never doubts his own abilities.

God knows he can deliver you. So, when it's hard to see, let that be your hope.

God knows he can.

And God will.

LISTEN
You're Gonna Be OK
by Brian and Jenn Johnson

Starting Point

Psalm 138:7-8

"Though I walk in the midst of trouble, you preserve me against the wrath of my enemies. You stretch out your hand, and your right hand delivers me. The LORD will fulfill his purpose for me."

Today, may you know without a doubt **who** you are and ***whose*** you are. You are loved and you are God's. You are his creation and he claims you as his child.

When the days are dark, please remember what is true about you: You are loved and cherished. Nothing can change that. God will never stop loving you or coming for you.

This is your starting point for the life of healing and deliverance: Believe that YOU ARE LOVED.

Then…

Lean into God's love for you every day, **_especially_** on the days when temptation is strong. Let the Lord's love for you strengthen you into making wise and healthy decisions.

Practice listening for the Lord every day. How do you do this? By reading and meditating on Scripture. Choose a verse or two that resonates with you or that encourages you (the verses above would work great for this), and repeat it in your mind. Carry it with you through the day by repeating it whenever you feel anxious, tempted, or distressed. Repeat it as you fall asleep believing that it is true for you.

As you stand in God's love and grace, purge anything unhealthy or false from your life. Then REPLACE the unhealthy thoughts with renewed thoughts and allow the healing work of the Holy Spirit to flood into your life. Your behaviors will be transformed as a result.

Today, I encourage you to pray in Jesus' name for healing. His name alone has the power to strengthen, heal, and save. Be specific about the healing you need and choose to wait patiently for the Lord to work.

LISTEN

Mention of Your Name

by Brian and Jenn Johnson

Darkness, Flee.

Darkness, you have to flee.
You are taking up space that is
not yours to occupy.

You are taking up space in my heart,
you are taking up space in my mind,
and you have no right to be there.

You must flee because I claim this day
the light of Christ.
I claim you, Jesus, for my heart and mind.

I have given in to the
weight of darkness for too long.
Jesus, be my light so I can see a way forward.

It's been dark for a while now,
and I have been losing hope.
Do not let me be overcome by this darkness.

May you shine your beautiful light into my heart!
Shine it brightly, and reveal to me my sins

so that I can wholeheartedly
confess them before you.

Shine your radiant light in me
so I can be a light bearer.
Don't let me be just another
basket over your light!

Shine so brightly in me that others
will be able to see you.
Jesus, empower me with your Holy Spirit.

You are who I need.
Drive out the darkness!
Deliver me from it!
Do not let me be just another
casualty of darkness!

Beautiful Savior,
you came into this broken world to redeem and save.
Do not let me live as if you have not come.

"I have come into the world as a light, so that no one who believes in
me should stay in darkness."
John 12:46

Encouragement and Community

Hebrews 10:24-25

"And let us consider how to provoke one another to love and good deeds, not neglecting to meet together as is the habit of some, but encouraging one another, and all the more as you see the Day approaching."

Who can you encourage today? It doesn't have to be big or weird. Even small statements like, "Hey, you did _____ really well," can go a long way to encourage the heart of another.

There is something powerful about speaking encouragement to another person. Encouraging others not only makes them feel good, but it makes you feel good! It strengthens you both! So be generous with your kind words and encouragement, and you will soon find your joy increasing as a result.

On a related note: Don't isolate yourself from others, especially when you are feeling down.

"…not neglecting to meet together…"

One tactic the enemy of our souls uses to keep us down and feeling worse about ourselves is to isolate us from others. He wants to isolate us from healthy, God-centered community so that the lies he is speaking over us will sound more and more like truth.

Do not be deceived. We need other people. We especially need other people who are a part of the believing community of faith. Be brave and diligent, and connect with a strong community of believers so that you can be encouraged and strengthened in God's love and truth.

Take a moment and name at least one friend you can reach out to and connect with today.

Is there a community (a campus ministry, a church or youth group, etc.) that you need to reconnect with or be more intentional with?

What are one or two practical steps you can take today to connect with others?

LISTEN
Love Will Hold You, by Katie Heckel

Rest

Matthew 11:28-30

"Come to me, all you that are weary and are carrying heavy burdens, and I will give you rest. Take my yoke upon you, and learn from me; for I am gentle and humble in heart, and you will find rest for your souls. For my yoke is easy, and my burden is light."

Right now you are weary and your burden is heavy. So, you are who Jesus is addressing when he says, "Come to me ... and you will find rest."

On the days when your load is heavy, envision yourself unloading every worry, every fear, every doubt, and every pain onto Jesus. Our Lord may be gentle and humble, but he is also STRONG.

His gentleness and humility are what make it possible for us to unload our burdens on him. The Lord's strength is what holds us up when we are too weak to carry ourselves.

May you enter into this sweet rest today.
And remember. You are loved.

Visualization Practice: Picture a burden you are carrying and name it. Now, imagine that you have been carrying it around like a heavy backpack. Feel the burden of it. Be aware of the weight that is bearing down on you. Now imagine that you are taking that backpack off, slipping one arm out from under the straps at a time. Hear it thud to the ground. Picture Jesus, arms outstretched, ready to receive your burden. Place it in his hands and watch as he straps it on himself. Notice how strong he is. Notice how he doesn't crumble under the weight of it. Notice how light you feel knowing that he understands and knows about the burden you have been carrying. Talk to him about it and thank him that he has taken it from you.

Can you make some time today to rest? Maybe you'll find time for a brief nap, or a long one if you need it. Perhaps you'll rest by resting your mind. Go for a walk or simply sit outside and enjoy the weather. Find something that is truly restful for you that has nothing to do with videos, games, or social media. Unplug from technology and connect with your Savior. Find him and you will find rest.

NEED HELP RELAXING?

Go to https://www.exploringpeace.com/podcast.html and use these relaxation meditations by Whitney Simpson to calm and relax your body, mind, and spirit.

Tomorrow Will Be Better

BY MELODY SIMMS

I'm tired.

Of playing around,

Of allowing other things to come before you,

Of feeling like a failure,

Of getting to the end of each day and promising myself that tomorrow will be different.

I want what you have for me.

I take your gift—I shake it, inspect it, pick at the beautiful wrapping job—and then quickly dismiss it, deciding once again to keep the already opened, comfortable, self-loathing mess.

This moment right now—THIS ONE—let me cling to it. Let me hold so tight to this moment where I so strongly feel your presence. Where I know your realness and would fight to the death anything that tried to take you from me.

I don't want to get into this tainted day, this tainted world and trade in these truths—trade in the truth of my security in you for a quick fix.

I don't want to continue to assess myself based on the coming and goings of my feelings, of my whims.
Rather Lord, I want - scratch that - I NEED every second of every day to cling to the truth that you are the only way out of this pit. You are the only way out of these chains that pull at me so heavily.

You. I need you. I want you. I must have you as close to me as possible at every moment. This is the only way I can walk through this broken world and keep any form of hope.

Dear God, when I try to break away, please don't let me. Whatever you need to do, do it.

In this untainted moment of peace—this beautiful assurance that comes with knowing you are Lord of my life, you are my Savior, you are my strength and my source—hold me so tight that I can't even begin to think about pulling away from you.

When things of this world try so hard to distract me and tell me things I know aren't true, press into me so that I can't get away. Hold onto my hand that tries to break your grip, that insists I know best and insists that tomorrow I can try again.

Take the word tomorrow from my mouth, my mind, my comprehension.

Today I'm yours.

Today you hold me.

Today I will not waste.

Today is a gift. I refuse to take one more gift from you and pick at the beautiful outside without fully embracing what's on the inside.

I want to live for today, not tomorrow

Yet I Still Dare to Hope

Read over the following verses slowly and mindfully. Between each verse, take in a deep breath and then exhale slowly as you repeat what you just read to yourself.

Lamentations 3:19-32

"The thought of my affliction is bitter beyond words. I will never forget this awful time as I grieve over my loss. Yet I still dare to hope when I remember this: The steadfast love of the LORD never ceases.

(Breathe in, breathe out as you repeat these words to yourself: "The steadfast love of the LORD never ceases.")

His mercies never come to an end; they are new every morning;

(Breathe in, breathe out.)

Great is your faithfulness. The LORD is my inheritance; therefore, I will hope in him!

(Breathe in, breathe out.)

The LORD is good to those who wait on him—to those who search for him.
(Breathe in, breathe out.)

So, it is good to wait quietly for salvation from the LORD...

(Breathe in, breathe out.)

... for he will have compassion according to the abundance of his steadfast love."

(Breathe in, breathe out.)

The author of these verses was going through a terrible time. He felt terrible emotionally. He felt terrible physically. He felt terrible in the deepest parts of himself.

But he dug down deep past the emotions and grounded himself in this **greater reality**: God is faithful and God's love is steadfast and unfailing.

He let his mind settle on that truth instead of his circumstances or his feelings. He dared to hope and, therefore, was able to see that since God is faithful, and since God loved him, and since God's love never ends, he could wait on the LORD with a confident trust that God would deliver him from this awful time.

He settled in to the truth that God knew how to bring him into the good and full life that he wanted more than anything—a life of joy and peace and abundance.

Cling to that truth today for yourself: God is working. The LORD is and will always act on your behalf and for your good. God will rescue you from this terrible time.

God will redeem this terrible time.

God will bring you into your best life.

And then this time will become a time you look back on and say, "That's when I learned how faithful and loving and able my God is. That's when I learned about God's compassion and grace. That's when my healing began—when I dared to hope."

LISTEN
Shelter, by Vertical Worship

Psalm 139:7-12

Where can I go from your Spirit? Where can I flee from your presence? If I go up to the heavens, you are there; if I make my bed in the depths, you are there. If I rise on the wings of the dawn, if I settle on the far side of the sea, even there your hand will guide me, your right hand will hold me fast.

If I say, "Surely the darkness will hide me and the light become night around me," even the darkness will not be dark to you; the night will shine like day, for darkness is as light to you.

When I awake, I am still with you.

Waiting

Psalm 40:1-3

"I waited patiently for the LORD; he turned to me and heard my cry. He lifted me out of the slimy pit, out of the mud and mire; he set my feet on a rock and gave me a firm place to stand. He put a new song in my mouth, a hymn of praise to our God!"

Philippians 1:6

"I am confident of this, that the one who began a good work in you will bring it to completion by the day of Jesus Christ."

You're in a time of waiting.

You're waiting for healing to come, waiting for strength to come, waiting for answers and relief to come. But even in this time, when it's so hard and your patience is running thin, God is doing a good work in you.

I know it's hard to see it now when everything is so dark, so heavy, so clouded. But it's true. *"The one who began a good work in you will be faithful to complete it."*

You will get to the other side.

You will sing a new song, one of joy.

You will.

And your God will sing it with you.

But what does waiting look like, really? Does it look like sitting around twiddling your thumbs, being helpless to do anything until someone comes to save you? Certainly not. Waiting on the Lord simply means holding on to the hope and expectation that he will act on your behalf.

Don't be passive in the meantime. Do what you can do to bring light and joy into your life while you wait on the Lord to do what only he can do. So, while you wait, do what is good for you. Bring healthy things into your mind and your body, and interact in healthy ways with others.

"Keep on doing the things that you have learned and received and heard and seen in me, and the God of peace will be with you." ~Philippians 4:9

Keep on doing what you know is good and good for you. Today, that may mean that you simply rest. Tomorrow it may mean that you take a walk. The next day it might mean to take a break from social media. Take each day one day at a time. Do the next right thing each day, and the God of peace will be with you.

What is one practical thing you can do today that is good for you? Write it below. Then commit to making it happen.

LISTEN
Anchor, by Skillet

Remember to Breathe

Think about your breath for a moment. Just pause for a moment and focus on it. Don't change anything about it, just pay attention to its coming and going.

Paying attention to your breath and using your breath to calm you down when you are anxious is an extremely important practice. You see, when we feel anxious, our breath becomes shallow and quick raising our heart rate and communicating a false message to our minds that we are in danger, trouble is at hand, and fear is appropriate. If we don't do something to change this, we may soon find ourselves in a state of panic. Taking control of our breath by taking deep, mindful inhales and then slow, cleansing exhales, can be enough to calm our minds and slow our heart rate.

Not only can focusing on your breath help you physically, it's also a great way to strengthen you spiritually. Consider how your breath is the source of your life. You must breathe in order to live. Now, consider what Genesis 2:7 tells us:
"...then the LORD God formed man from the dust of the ground and breathed into his nostrils the breath of life; and the man became a living being."

27

With every breath we take, we are connecting to the source of our life. Not oxygen, but the very Spirit of God. The LORD God is the source of your life. It is the LORD's breath within you that sustains you and gives you energy.

Out of nothingness God created our beautiful and amazing world. Out of darkness and chaos God brought forth light and order and beauty. The LORD will do the same for you and in you. Out of your nothingness, your chaos, your emptiness, God will breathe and create light and beauty and life in you.

Every time you connect with your breath, you're connecting to the Source of love itself: God. God is love. Out of Love came your life. So every time you breathe in, remember that God is breathing his love into you.

You are loved.

You are seen.

You are cared for.

You are heard.

You are never forgotten.

Breathe deep of this Love, and exhale in peace knowing that your life is precious and sourced by the God of the universe who is your healing, your nourishment, your peace, and your restoration.

BREATHING PRACTICE

If you feel anxious, try using a 4:8 ratio breath. Breathe in for four counts, hold for a count at the top of your breath, and exhale for eight counts. This breathing pattern will slow your heart rate and help calm your mind. Focus solely on your breath. When other thoughts intrude, notice them and then quickly tell them they are dismissed for now.

You can also incorporate breath prayers into this breathing practice. Choose a name of God that you connect with (Jesus, Lord, Father, etc.). As you breathe in, say his name and as you exhale state a truth about him (you are good, you love me, etc.), or make a request (help me, be with me, etc.). Practice this until you sense yourself feeling calmer.

LISTEN
You Won't Let Go, by Cory Asbury

God Is at Peace with You

Isaiah 35:3-4

"Strengthen the feeble hands, steady the knees that give way, say to those with fearful hearts, 'Be strong, do not fear; Your God will come, he will come with vengeance; with divine retribution he will come to save you.'"

John 10:10

"The thief comes only to steal and kill and destroy. I came that they may have life, and have it abundantly."

When the voice in your mind tells you that you are not valuable or that your life does not have worth, you can be sure of one thing: That is not the voice of God. That is the voice of your enemy whose only goal is to "steal, kill and destroy" (John 10:10). But God will come with vengeance against the enemy of your soul and he will have to flee.

So, when those thoughts arise, say confidently to yourself, "God is at peace with me." Stand in the truth that God loves you and calls you friend. The Lord sees you as a valuable and precious child of worth.

Say this to yourself:
"God is at peace with me. The Lord's opinion of me is what matters."

God is at peace with you. In the power of the Spirit, God will enable you to be at peace with yourself and see yourself the way he sees you.

Love yourself.
Be kind to yourself.
You are precious and of great value.

BREATHING PRACTICE: Take a few minutes to sit in silence and take slow, deep breaths, exhaling slowly and gently. Be aware of God's presence with you. Imagine the Lord sitting with you and smiling. Sit in awareness of his great love for you. Breathe in that love, and exhale any thoughts or feelings that are negative and not full of love. Then thank God for loving you always.

LISTEN
Be Kind to Yourself, by Andrew Peterson

The Truest Thing About You

The truest thing about you is not what people say, what they think, what they do, or how they treat you. Other people are walking around with their own pain and baggage, and the hurtful things they say are not about you as much as they are a tell-tale sign of the place they're in. Don't let someone else's bad day become your identity.

The truest thing about you is not how you feel. Feelings ebb and flow and often do not tell an accurate story. Feelings exaggerate. Feelings lie. They fill in the gaps to stories you have no facts for, and often you're the one who loses in that story. Don't give your feelings that much power. They are not the truest thing about you.

The truest thing about you is not your circumstances, your shattered heart, the broken promise, the disappointment and pain. Things happen—sometimes good, sometimes not. They are not the truest thing about you.

Even your worst mistakes and failures are not the truest thing about you. Should you confess those things? Do they need forgiveness? You bet. But not even those things are the truest thing about you. They are not your identity.

The truest thing about you is that you belong to God.

The LORD created you, formed you, and knit you together. (Psalm 139:13-14). Like a Good Shepherd God watches over you. Not one moment or breath goes unnoticed by him.

The truest thing about you is that you have a Savior.

Everything that has been said to you and everything that has been said by you, everything that has been done to you, and everything that has been done by you—every hurt feeling, painful experience, and devastating loss— is redeemed by what the Lord says and what the Lord has done.

You are redeemed.
You are bought back.
You are loved.

So clear your mind. Listen to God's voice. Change the habit of negative self-talk into the habit of remembering what is true about you.

Speak this truth to yourself.
Say it LOUD if you must!
Write it down over and over again.

I am a child of God. I am loved.

Forgive yourself.
Give yourself grace.
Begin loving yourself because you are worth loving.

You are worth forgiving,
you are worth redeeming,
and your life is worth living.

But God loves who we really are—whether we like it or not... His love, which calls us into existence, calls us to come out of self-hatred and to step into His truth. "Come to me now," Jesus says. "Acknowledge and accept who I want to be for you: A Savior of boundless compassion, infinite patience, unbearable forgiveness, and love that keeps no score of wrongs. Quit projecting onto Me your own feelings about yourself. At this moment your life is a bruised reed, and I will not crush it; a smoldering wick, and I will not quench it. You are in a safe place."[5]

-Brennan Manning

---

[5] Brennan Manning, *Abba's Child—The Cry of the Heart for Intimate Belonging* (Colorado Springs, CO: NavPress, 2015), 6

Shift Your Gaze

Psalm 121

"I lift my eyes to the hills—where does my help come from? My help comes from the LORD, the maker of heaven and earth. He will not let your foot slip—he who watches over you will not slumber; indeed, he who watches over Israel will neither slumber nor sleep. The LORD watches over you—the LORD is your shade at your right hand; the sun will not harm you by day nor the moon by night. The LORD will keep you from all harm— He will watch over your life; the LORD will watch over your coming and going both now and forevermore."

When was the last time you let your "eyes" gaze upon God? When was the last time you just allowed your mind to be full of the Lord, totally focused on him and his love for you—even for a few moments?

I have to constantly remind myself to do this when I am anxious, depressed, stressed, fearful, or worried because when I don't focus on the Lord my natural response is to begin problem-solving in my own strength which requires a lot of mental energy. However, I am a better problem-solver when I let God do the work of solving. **And that happens when I shift my gaze and look to the Lord.** When I do that, I remember that the Lord can do all things, which includes holding me up through the most difficult times.

Look up today.

Remind yourself Who is on your side.

> *"I can do all things through Christ who strengthens me."*
> Philippians 4:13

Make a list of three things that make your God a capable ally.

LISTEN
Oh My Soul, by Casting Crowns

Psalm 3

1 O, LORD, how many are my foes! Many are rising against me; 2 many are saying to me, "There is no help for you in God." 3 But you, O LORD, are a shield around me, my glory, and the One who lifts up my head. 4 I cry aloud to the LORD, and he answers me from his holy hill. 5 I lie down to sleep; I wake again, for the LORD sustains me. 6 I am not afraid of ten thousands of people who have set themselves against me all around. 7 Rise up, O LORD! Deliver me, O my God! For you strike all my enemies on the cheek; you break the teeth of the wicked. 8 Deliverance belongs to the LORD; may your blessing be on your people!

God Is My Help

Psalm 63:1, 5-7

"O God, you are my God, I seek you, my soul thirsts for you; my flesh faints for you, as in a dry and weary land where there is no water... My soul is satisfied as with a rich feast, and my mouth praises you with joyful lips when I think of you on my bed and meditate on you in the watches of the night; For you have been my help, and in the shadow of your wings I sing for joy."

Turn back a page and re-read Psalm 3, or look it up in your own Bible. Read it slowly, taking it verse by verse.

Now, look at verses 1 and 2. What are the Psalmist's foes saying to him? Write it below.

Now, look in verse 3. There are three things the Psalmist says about God in response to his enemies. Write them below.

Look closely at verses 4-6. The Psalmist gives a testimony to what he knows is true about the LORD because of his personal experience:

I cry aloud to the LORD, and he **answers** me.

I lie down and sleep; I wake again, for the LORD **sustains** me.

And because of this…

I am not afraid.

Even though his enemies told him otherwise, even in his pain, the Psalmist (David) stated what he knew was true about God.

In the Psalm 63 passage above, David remembers how God has been his help, and it moves him to praise and thanksgiving. "…*my mouth praises you with joyful lips when I think of you on my bed and meditate on you in the watches of the night;* **For you have been my help**, *and in the shadow of your wings I sing for joy.*"

Try this exercise as you consider the truth that God is **your** help. Create an acronym for HELP such as…

He

Embraces me with

Love and

Provides

Play around with it and come up with your own acronym for HELP.

H

E

L

P

A great prayer to pray when you feel trapped, lost, worried, or alone is "Jesus, help me." It's a powerful prayer. When we call on Jesus' name, he hears every time, and he comes to rescue us. His coming may be as subtle as a whisper, or it may be a profound spiritual or emotional experience. Whatever you need, that is what Jesus brings when you cry out to him. He is your Help, and he never fails. Believe that today. The LORD is an ever-present Help in trouble.

LISTEN
Rescue, by Lauren Daigle

Do Not Worry - Part 1

Matthew 6:25-34

"Therefore I tell you, do not worry about your life, what you will eat or what you will drink, or about your body, what you will wear. Is not life more than food, and the body more than clothing? Look at the birds of the air; they neither sow nor reap nor gather into barns, and yet your heavenly Father feeds them. Are you not of more value than they? And can any of you by worrying add a single hour to your span of life? And why do you worry about clothing? Consider the lilies of the field, how they grow; they neither toil nor spin, yet I tell you, even Solomon in all his glory was not clothed like one of these.

But if God so clothes the grass of the field, which is alive today and tomorrow is thrown into the oven, will he not much more clothe you—you of little faith? Therefore do not worry, saying, 'What will we eat?' or 'What will we drink?' or 'What will we wear?' For it is the Gentiles who strive for all these things; and indeed your heavenly Father knows that you need all these things. But strive first for the kingdom of God and his righteousness, and all these things will be given to you as well.

"So do not worry about tomorrow, for tomorrow will bring worries of its own. Today's trouble is enough for today."

Worry is something that grips all of us, and it can become a major problem, disrupting our ability to focus and robbing us of sleep. But here in Matthew 6 Jesus says in no uncertain terms, "Do not worry about your life…" He doesn't say, "Therefore I present to you an option you may choose to consider." No, he is clear and concise and says, "Do not worry."

How could Jesus say something like this? Was he out of touch with reality? Did he not see everything that goes on in the world that can cause us to tremble with fear and anxiety?

No, he was not out of touch. In fact, he was very in touch with the reality of this broken world. He was born into poverty, lived the first part of his life as a refugee because a crazed king wanted to kill him, and the more truth he told about who he was and his mission, the more those in authority wanted him dead. No, Jesus understood the brokenness of the world and the treachery of people. He was well acquainted with grief and sorrow (Isaiah 53:3). He was well aware of what kept people up at night robbing them of sleep, peace, and a sense of safety.

And yet he said, *"Do not worry about your life… can any of you by worrying add a single hour to your span of life?"* The implied answer is a resounding, "No." Worrying is a futile action. Instead, Jesus asks us to look around and notice the creatures and the creation that daily rest secure in the loving care of the Father.

Look at the birds! You are of more value to your Father than the birds, and he takes perfect care of them. Look at the lilies of the field! Their lives are so fleeting, so temporary, and yet God clothes them with stunning beauty. Your life is of infinite value and worth, so much more than the lilies of the field. HOW MUCH MORE, then, will your Heavenly Father see you, understand your needs, care for you, and provide for you?

So, for today, focus on this truth:

You are valuable.

Yes YOU.

YOU are a valuable person of worth created by God to love and be loved. Your existence matters. Please believe me. And God is your good Father who will take care of you.

Be at peace today.

MEDITATION PRACTICE: Look up and read Psalm 23. Slow down and meditate on a line or phrase that speaks to you. Make this Psalm your prayer to God today.

LISTEN
Sparrows and Lilies, by Pat Barrett

Do Not Worry - Part 2

Matthew 6:34

"So do not worry about tomorrow, for tomorrow will bring worries of its own. Today's trouble is enough for today."

How can we set worry aside? Or better yet, how can we replace the habit of worry with a more effective way of coping with anxiety? Here's an idea:

When your brain starts to create scenarios, and you think you must figure out a solution to every worst-case ending that your anxious mind dreams up, try changing your focus.

Instead of playing the "What if" game: *"If this happens, then I will_____"*, flip the switch, change the story that's being created and say, **"*Even if* *this happens,* God *will* _____."**

Then, state what you know God will do even in the face of difficulty or pain:

God will never leave me. (Deut. 31:6)
God will take care of me. (Matt. 6)

God will comfort me. (2 Cor. 1:3)

God will keep loving me. (1 John 3:1)

And on and on … you get the picture.

This practice takes the focus off the "What ifs,", which are nothing more than stories created with little to no facts that make you responsible for saving yourself if something terrible happens. It places your focus back on God and what the Lord is capable of doing. It reminds you that there is NOTHING God can't handle and NOWHERE the Lord is unwilling to go for you.

There is no need to play the "What if" game. I've been there, done that; and I can tell you that it leads nowhere good. It actually leads you precisely **nowhere**. It only serves to keep you stuck and make you exhausted. In addition, many of the horrible scenarios I imagined in my deepest anxiety never happened. But even if your worst fears do come true, God will be present to help and comfort.

This may take some practice. It's a skill that you will need to develop. It will take some time to get rid of the old habit of worry and replace it with trust in your Father, but you can do it.

God is there for you, always. God will act on your behalf and in your best interest. God is holding you. God is with you. So do not worry.

Be at peace today.

Fill in the blanks here or in a journal to start changing the storyline in your mind over something you are worrying about. Write as many "Even if" statements as you need.

Even if _____, God will _____.

LISTEN
Enough, by Elias Dummer

Give Thanks for God's Goodness

Read Psalm 103:1-5

"Bless the LORD, O my soul, and all that is within me, bless his holy name. Bless the LORD, O my soul, and do not forget all his benefits—who forgives all your iniquity, who heals all your diseases, who redeems your life from the Pit, who crowns you with steadfast love and mercy, who satisfies you with good as long as you live so that your youth is renewed like the eagle's." (New Revised Standard Version)

Read the passage again from the New Living Translation:

"Let all that I am praise the LORD; with my whole heart, I will praise his holy name. Let all that I am praise the LORD; may I never forget the good things he has done for me. He forgives all my sins and heals my diseases. He redeems me from death and crowns me with love and tender mercies. He fills my life with good things. My youth is renewed like the eagle's."

I like reading passages in different translations because it helps them come alive to me a little more. For today my encouragement to you is to read this, and then for each action it says God takes, think about how the LORD has taken that action—or IS taking that action—in your life. (If it helps you focus, you can underline the actions of God you see in the passage.)

And if you can't see how the LORD is working, or if there is still a place you need him to act, ask him to do it.

And REMEMBER.

Remember how God has been good to you in the past and then know that, because he never changes, the LORD will continue to act on your behalf to forgive, heal, redeem, and crown you with love and mercy, filling your life with good.

Thank God for that.
Thank God for being good.
Thank God for being good to you.

Be at peace today.

Remembering is essential to your faith. When it's dark and heavy it's hard to see and feel God's goodness. But, if you remember and give thanks regularly, then you can go back to how he has been faithful and cling to that when you are struggling. So remember and give thanks when the days are brighter so you will be sustained in the dark.

54

What can you remember and give God thanks for today?
Write some things below.

LISTEN
Goodness of God, by Bethel Music, Jenn
Johnson

God looks at us and says,
"You are my dear, dear child;
I'm delighted with you."

-NT Wright

A Blessing for You

Psalm 86:8-10

"There is none like you among the gods, O LORD, nor are there any works like yours. All the nations you have made shall come and bow down before you, O LORD, and shall glorify your name. For you are great and do wondrous things; you alone are God."

Ephesians 3:14-19

"I pray that, according to the riches of his glory, he may grant that you may be strengthened in your inner being with power through his Spirit, and that Christ may dwell in your hearts through faith, as you are being rooted and grounded in love. I pray that you may have the power to comprehend with all the saints, what is the breadth and length and height and depth, and to know the love of Christ that surpasses knowledge, so that you may be filled with all the fullness of God."

There is just something about knowing that someone is praying for you and speaking blessing over your life. Please receive this blessing today. Take it in, and imagine the Holy Spirit gazing upon you and smiling. God loves you. God will never leave you. He is the God who saves.

May the **God of PEACE** calm your body and mind today.

May the **God who PROTECTS** be your shield and guard you from the enemy.

May the **God of CLARITY** bring focus to your mind and help you see what's true.

May the **God of JOY** put a smile on your face today.

May the **God who is LIGHT** cast out all darkness that surrounds you.

May the **God of LOVE** fill your heart so you know how loved you truly are.

May the **God who SAVES** lift you up and enable you to stand.

What would you ask of God today? Feel free to write your own additions to the blessing above. Tell God what you need.

LISTEN
Love Like This, by Lauren Daigle

The Lord Knows How

Psalm 146:8-9

"The LORD sets the prisoners free; the LORD opens the eyes of the blind. The LORD lifts up those who are bowed down; the LORD loves the righteous. The LORD watches over the strangers; he upholds the orphan and the widow..."

Whenever you begin to feel like you must be the solver of all the problems, the figure-outer of all things confusing or stressful, remember this passage. The people of Israel were faced with real issues that made life challenging and stressful. But notice who the Psalmist says is in charge of solving, helping, rescuing, watching over. It's the LORD. So, we don't have to take all of that responsibility upon ourselves and figure out every problem in our own strength or wisdom.

The LORD knows how. The LORD saves, lifts up, loves, watches over, upholds, protects, opens eyes. So *"cast all your anxiety on him for he cares for you"* (1 Peter 5:7). The LORD knows how. You don't have to know and solve. The LORD will direct your steps and teach you what to say, how to say it, and will give you peace and power—everything you need.
Remember this: The LORD knows how.

Be at peace today.

Is there some problem you are trying to solve all on your own?
Name it below.

Write or say a brief prayer asking God to give you his wisdom.

LISTEN
 Water and Dust by Cory Asbury

Rejoice, Pray, Give Thanks

1 Thessalonians 5:16-22

"Rejoice always, pray without ceasing, give thanks in all circumstances; for this is the will of God in Christ Jesus for you. Do not quench the Spirit. Do not despise the words of prophets, but test everything; hold fast to what is good; abstain from every form of evil."

REJOICE

"Rejoice always…"

What is one thing today you can be glad over? Intentionally smile when you think of this. It may be a person, a relationship, a hobby, or a book. Maybe you will think of God and how good the Lord is. Hold this thought in your mind and smile.

Why smile? Because smiling actually tells your brain you are happy! "The fact is… a smile spurs a chemical reaction in the brain, releasing certain hormones including dopamine and serotonin. Dopamine increases our feelings of happiness. Serotonin release is associated with reduced stress."[6]

PRAY

"…pray without ceasing…"

Is the phrase "pray without ceasing" supposed to be yet another burden on us? Not at all. This isn't about "do more and pray right so God will like you, hear you, and answer you." Rather, it's an open invitation and reminder that you have constant, never-ending, personal, one-on-one access to the God of the universe, the God who loves you, sees you, and helps you in everything.

When the negative thoughts want to take up all the space in your mind, keep replacing them with different thoughts. In addition, fill your mind with good thoughts—about you, about God.

A prayer as simple as *"Jesus, tell me what's true,"* or *"Speak your truth over me,"* is great. I use both of these regularly because my own thoughts sometimes tend to lean toward beating myself down.

GIVE THANKS

"…give thanks in all circumstances…"

By giving thanks you are holding in your mind what is good. This will help you rejoice, and it is also a way to pray. So, by giving thanks regularly, you are able to rejoice always and pray without ceasing!

---

[6]Spector, N. (2018, January 10). Smiling Can Trick Your Brain into Happiness - and Boost Your Health. Retrieved July 17, 2020, from https://www.nbcnews.com/better/health/smiling-can-trick-your-brain-happiness-boost-your-health ncna822591

Be at peace today as you remember the blessings in your life and the good things about yourself. And smile about it! You'll feel better.

LISTEN
Yet Will I Praise You by Passion, Crowder

Whatever Is...

Philippians 4:8-9

"Whatever is true, whatever is honorable, whatever is just, whatever is pure, whatever is pleasing, whatever is commendable, if there is any excellence and if there is anything worthy of praise, think about these things. Keep on doing the things you have learned and received and heard and seen in me, and the God of peace will be with you."

Focus on each phrase of this verse one at a time. Underline the object of "whatever is." For instance, "Whatever is <u>true</u>…"

In these few lines, the Apostle Paul has given us an extremely helpful list to guide us toward what kinds of things we should set our minds on. "Whatever is…

TRUE… HONORABLE… JUST… PURE… PLEASING… COMMENDABLE… EXCELLENT… WORTHY OF PRAISE

So, before you set your eyes and your thoughts on certain things, ask yourself:

Is this true?

Is this honorable?

Is this pure, and is it pleasing to God?

Is it commendable, excellent, or worthy of praise?

Here's a hint: If you need to hide it, it's not.

What we set our minds on will impact how we feel and the decisions we make. If you are finding it hard to feel good about yourself or to enjoy life, please consider what you are bringing into your mind and how those messages or images are affecting your thoughts.

Listen to the Apostle Paul's encouragement from Colossians 3:16.

"Let the word of God dwell in you richly; teach and admonish one another in all wisdom, and with gratitude in your hearts sing psalms, hymns, and spiritual songs to God."

Take some time to write a prayer to God. Talk to the Lord honestly about what you are bringing into your mind and how those things are affecting you. Don't be afraid. You can be honest with God, and it will help you to write some things down.

Is there something you need to stop doing or viewing? What is it?

Is there someone who can hold you accountable to this?

How would you go about asking this person to do so?

What is something you can fill your mind with **today** and future days that will encourage you and lift you up in God's truth? Write one thing down that you will do today.

LISTEN
Found, by Chris Renzema

Too Far Gone?

Out of the pit God will lift you up.
The LORD's salvation is here!
Yahweh's hand reaches down to save you.

Look up!
Take hold!
See his face!

And if you can't reach your hand up—if your strength fails you
so that all you can do is whisper God's name and acknowledge
his presence—that is enough.

God will descend to your depths,
lift you out of that pit,
and hold you until you can stand on your own.

The LORD will hold you and never grow tired.

GOD WILL NEVER GROW TIRED OF YOU.

In your weakness God sees you,
God loves you.
God delights in you even when you are the most broken.

And as you are held in God's gaze—

being loved for simply existing—
your strength will come.

Because God's love heals you.
It is a balm for your wounds.
It is a balm for your soul.

Be healed my child.
You are greatly loved.
You are not too far gone.

LISTEN

Ezekiel 36:36

Then the nations that are left all around you shall know that I, the LORD, have rebuilt the ruined places, and replanted that which was desolate; I, the LORD have spoken, and I will do it.

Suggested Practices to Soothe, Calm, and Relax You

Take a soothing bath.

Hug a friend or family member.

Pet or play with your dog or cat.

Enjoy a good meal or a favorite drink such as tea or hot chocolate. Eat your favorite ice cream or piece of candy. Take the time to really savor and enjoy the tastes. The key is to enjoy, not to overindulge. So, eat or drink slowly and in moderation.

Watch a sunset.

Create a room or a space in your room that is filled with things that you enjoy or that calm you. You can decorate it with pictures and art that bring you joy and that are pleasing to the eye. You can fill it with comfy pillows and blankets that have a soothing feel to them. You can put encouraging scriptures or messages on the walls or in a journal that you'll keep in that space. Have fun and make this *your* space of joy and beauty. When you are distressed, go into this space and reconnect with what is true and calming.

Listen to music that brings you joy or that is calming, relaxing—and, if it has lyrics, songs that have a positive message.

Bake something you love and that smells good.

Light a candle that smells good to you or put some good-smelling oils in a diffuser. (Lavender is great for creating a relaxing and calming vibe.)

Go outside or open a window and focus on the sounds you hear. Focus on the details of those sounds. Next, focus on something pleasant that you see in nature.

Listen to a guided meditation. A great resource for this can be found at **https://www.exploringpeace.com/podcast.html**.

Clean up the clutter. A messy or cluttered living space may actually increase your stress. Do a little cleaning and de-cluttering and enjoy the peace it brings.

Do something kind for another person or take part in a service project. Serving others takes our minds off ourselves and what is bothering us. Loving and serving others is just good medicine!

Scan to get to the Exploring Peace Meditations.

How to Use Visualization Techniques to Connect with God

When we are stressed, anxious, or depressed, praying can be very difficult. Please know that this is normal and you should not let that become an additional burden for you. However, connecting with God during our times of intense emotional pain or stress is crucial to finding comfort and healing. So, if words don't come or if we just don't know what to say, what can we do?

One method I like to use is visualization. God gifted us with beautiful minds that are capable of picturing our thoughts when we are incapable of finding the right words. I use this when I need to calm down, or when I need to simply stop talking and just BE STILL in the presence of the Lord. Below is one of my common visualization practices:

Jesus and I are sitting next to each other under a large tree. I am leaning on Jesus with my head on his shoulder and his arm is around me. There's a lake in front of us and we're gazing out at the water. A hillside lies just beyond the lake covered in trees. It's a sunny day, but not hot, and we're sheltered by the shade of the large tree we're sitting under. We just sit together, looking at the water. I'm smiling and content—and so is Jesus. I rest in the truth that he loves me, is not hurried, and is enjoying my presence and my love every bit as much as I am enjoying his.

Whatever image or scene you imagine, stay there in the moment with Jesus. You can begin to tell him what is on your mind while you are in that safe place with him. This can be a very powerful way to pray, but don't be discouraged if you don't feel you are "good" at it in the beginning. Keep practicing. You will notice that you're able to stay in those quiet moments for longer periods of time, and you will come away refreshed and renewed from being in the presence of the Lord.

Q&A with Stewart

Should I Tell Someone That I Am Struggling?

It's always wise to let a trusted friend, parent, or pastor know when you're experiencing difficulties. So many people struggle in silence when they don't need to do so. Sometimes what keeps people from telling another about their struggle is that they think the person won't understand, or they fear the person will make a big deal about it. They may also be afraid of being a burden to the person they tell.

Think carefully about who you will confide in. Choose someone you know to be wise and healthy. In other words, the friend who has a proven track record of unhealthy or unwise decisions is not the best choice. Also, just because someone can relate to what you're going through doesn't mean they can give you the help you need in your own struggle.

Should I Reach Out to a Therapist?

The difference between a therapist and other trusted adults, including pastors, is that a therapist is trained to understand mental health issues. They help people deal with problems like depression and anxiety every day. Pastors, parents, and good friends might be able to listen well, but they may not be able to offer you the type of trained guidance that a therapist can.

A sign that reaching out to a therapist would be helpful is when your emotional struggle begins to impact practical areas of your life such as your work, your studies, your relationships, and your physical health. So ask yourself whether you're noticing any of these issues:

- Struggles at school such as lower grades, attendance problems, frustrations with homework, or trouble concentrating

- Isolating yourself from others, not spending as much time with friends and family

- Sleep disruptions, whether that is sleeping a lot more than normal, sleeping a lot less than usual, or trouble going to sleep

- Panic attacks

- Low appetite or not wanting to eat

- Having thoughts of death or dying or wanting to hurt yourself

Am I Weird If I Am Struggling with Depression and/or Anxiety?

According to the *Anxiety and Depression Organization of America*, anxiety disorders are the most common mental illness in the

United States affecting forty million adults age eighteen and older each year. That's 18.1 percent of the population.[7]

Additionally, it's estimated that 6.7 percent of American adults have had at least one major depressive episode in a given year, and 16.5 percent of US youth between the ages of six and seventeen experienced a mental health disorder in 2016. That's 7.7 million teens.[8]

Finally, according to the advocacy group *One in Five Minds*, one in five youth age 18 and under struggle with a mental, behavioral, or emotional concern.[9] So, no, you are not weird, and you are definitely not alone.

Do I Need Medication?

Only a doctor or nurse practitioner can determine whether or not you need to be on medication for a mental health disorder. If your doctor does determine that medication would be helpful for you, it's important to have realistic expectations about how it can help.

---

[7] Facts & Statistics. (n.d.). Retrieved July 17, 2020, from https://adaa.org/about-adaa/press-room/facts-statistics

[8] Koskie, B. (1993, April 07). Depression: Facts, Statistics, and You. Retrieved July 17, 2020, from https://www.healthline.com/health/depression/facts-statistics-infographic

[9] One in Five Minds Advocates for Childrens Mental Health ... (n.d.). Retrieved July 17, 2020, from https://www.1in5minds.org/

The purpose of medication is to help you deal with depressive or anxious symptoms more effectively. It is not a "magic" pill that will solve all your problems and make every issue go away. Medication is most effective when paired with regular counseling. Additionally, medication is not a replacement for developing the skills you need to deal with the symptoms of depression and anxiety. A therapist can teach you how to manage difficult emotions when they come up and teach you how your thoughts impact your mood.

What If I Have Thoughts of Harming Myself?

If you have thoughts of harming yourself or have harmed yourself in some way, please tell a trusted adult immediately. Sometimes when you are in a dark place, practicing self-harm or even ending your life can seem like the only option. Self-harm is a sign that you have a lot of pain that isn't being dealt with and needs to be tended to. Acting on those thoughts will not make the pain go away. In other words, *pain is not a remedy for pain*. Getting those thoughts and feelings out in the open and letting someone wise into your situation can help you gain perspective, give you hope, and set you on the path to healing.

A Note to Parents of Children Struggling with Depression, Anxiety, or Other Mental Health Challenges

PRAY FOR YOUR CHILD

No one can pray for your child like you can. No one can pray for your child with the strength, love, fervor, passion, or desperation that you can. No one loves your child more than you. No one knows your child better than you do.

You brought that life into being. You carried your child's body in yours. You chose that child. You have comforted, nourished, and desired the best for your child. You have dreamed dreams for your child that no one else has over countless nights and days.

You've dried the tears. You've taught the lessons. You've given the discipline. You've provided the opportunities for your child to grow and develop. You're the one who has invested all of that in your child simply because that child is yours, and your love knows no bounds.

Therefore, no one else can take all of that life, all of those experiences, all of that knowing, and all of that love before the Father. Only you can do that. Others can and will pray, yes. Invite them in! But do not exclude yourself. Do not think yourself powerless. Your prayers are powerful and effective.

So name what you desire for your child. Name what healing you are asking for. Envision the joy you want to see on your child's face and hold it before the Lord. Ask, seek, knock, and don't give up.

Pray in the car. Pray in the shower. Pray in your bed. Pray in the morning. Pray at night. Pray with your child and when you're away from your child. Pray in Jesus' name against darkness and lies, and pray for the light of Christ to fill and surround your son or daughter.

See it. Believe it. Cling to hope in faith trusting and believing that the God and Father to whom you are praying loves your child more than you ever could.

Everything you know about your child, God knows more. He knows the deepest thoughts, attitudes, desires, and fears of your child's heart. God formed your child. God breathed the breath of life into your child. God declares that your son, your daughter, is very good. God's love for your child never fails.

So believe that the desires of your heart—as deep and sincere as they are—are vastly outweighed by God's love and desires. Bring all that you have to God in prayer. He will receive it as a fragrant offering pleasing to his senses, and your love will join with the Lord's love to surround, strengthen, and heal your child.

Consider this: When Moses was born, Pharaoh was on a rampage against the Hebrew people. He put out an edict declaring that all newborn sons should be thrown in the Nile and drowned. However, the writer of Hebrews tells us, *"By faith Moses was hidden by his parents for three months after his birth, because they saw that the child was beautiful; and they were not afraid of the king's edict"* (Hebrews 11:23). Moses' parents saw him the way no one else could—and what they saw was a beautiful life. They loved him with an indescribable love, so they hid him and protected him from the enemy.

Hide your child in your love. Wrap your son or daughter in prayer, and do not be afraid of the enemy that is seeking to devour him or her. And may the peace of God and the love of Jesus our Savior guard your heart and mind as you stand firm in prayer for the sake of your son or daughter.

BE A CALMING PRESENCE

Your child needs you more than you can comprehend right now. If he resists, press on. He is not resisting you. He is just in a struggle every day—possibly even every moment of every day. Struggle is what he knows. So do not be offended if he struggles with you.

Hold her. Hold her close in love, support, acceptance, grace. Hold her literally and physically. Pick her up off the floor or off of the bed, if necessary.

Your child's behavior may make you uncomfortable. It may rub against your own fears, your own weaknesses, your own demons, but do not let that get in the way of what your child needs. Your child needs you: Your voice, your love your encouragement, your promise to never leave—to journey through the dark valley with him.

When you're frustrated, lonely, and tired, get help, support, and love from a trusted source. But don't leave your child in her anguish because you're tired, or because you think it's too hard. It is hard. It is exhausting. But don't give up. Be strong in the Lord. Ground yourself in his Word. Strengthen yourself for the battle and **stand**. Stand for the child who is trusting that you will be there when he feels like he is nowhere—unseen, unheard, unimportant, unable to make it one more day.

BE AWARE

Knock on her door. Ask how her day was. Give her encouragement in her homework. Don't sit in front of the TV or phone and leave your child in an isolated state.

Listen. Speak *truth*. Speak *love*. Speak *grace*. Remind your child that his God is strong. Remind him that he is loved, and you are not going anywhere.

REACH OUT

Call the doctor. Find a therapist. Don't isolate yourselves from help. The enemy uses isolation to defeat us. So, reach out and be the advocate your child needs.

PRACTICE SELF-CARE

Do something for yourself. Take a nap. Practice yoga. Go for a walk. Lie in a hammock. Listen to music that calms your soul and gives you hope. Do what is soothing and uplifting to your heart, mind, and soul.

Finally, give yourself grace for not being perfect. Forgive yourself for losing your temper. Forgive yourself for every way you feel weak or like a failure. Offer yourself the same love and grace you are offering to your child. Be held by your God. Listen to his voice, and believe what you know to be true: *I will never leave you nor forsake you.*

You've got this.

Don't give up.

You're gonna be okay.

Online Resources

Visit the *Centre for Clinical Interventions*[10] website for some terrific resources that address various mental health issues such as anxiety, worry, rumination, and more. We have listed some we consider particularly helpful below.

What is Anxiety? – This resource will help you understand what anxiety is and how it affects you.

What is Depression? – This resource will help you understand depression and how it affects you.

What is Self-Compassion? – This resource will help you understand what self-compassion is and how to develop it.

---

[10] Looking After Yourself. (n.d.). Retrieved July 17, 2020, from https://www.cci.health.wa.gov.au/Resources/Looking-After-Yourself

Breathing Retraining - This resource walks you through how to retrain your breathing to help you calm down.

Progressive Muscle Relaxation - This resource will guide you through a common form of relaxation designed to reduce muscle tension.

Facts About Sleep – This resource will help you understand the stages of sleep, the role and function of sleep, and the effects of lack of sleep.

Sleep Hygiene – This resource will outline helpful practices to help you sleep better.

Safety Behaviors – This resource will help you identify behaviors you depend on to reduce fears and anxiety in the short-term, but may actually keep anxiety going in the long-term.

Unhelpful Thinking Styles – This resource describes a number of unhelpful thinking styles that can cause a great deal of emotional distress.

Thinking and Feeling – This resource explains how your thoughts influence your feelings.

Staying Healthy – This resource outlines things you can do in order to make the most of what you are learning so you can stay well or even gain extra improvement.

Made in the USA
Monee, IL
07 February 2021

59899508R00062